Money PTSD

Money PTSD

Matthew Petchinsky

1

Money PTSD: When Trauma Hijacks Your Finances

By: Matthew Petchinsky

Disclaimer

This book is provided for **educational, informational, and emotional support purposes only**. It is intended to explore the psychological, emotional, and behavioral impacts of financial trauma—sometimes referred to in this book as "Money PTSD"—and to offer insight, reflection, and supportive frameworks for understanding one's relationship with money.

This book **does not provide medical, psychological, psychiatric, financial, or legal advice**. It is **not a substitute for professional diagnosis, treatment, therapy, counseling, psychiatric care, financial planning, or crisis intervention**. Nothing contained within this book should be interpreted as diagnosing any mental health condition, including post-traumatic stress disorder (PTSD), anxiety disorders, depression, or any other psychological or neurological condition.

The term "Money PTSD" as used in this book is a **descriptive and educational concept**, not a clinical diagnosis. Experiences described herein may resemble symptoms associated with trauma, stress, or anxiety, but only a **qualified licensed professional** can diagnose or treat mental health conditions.

Readers are strongly encouraged to seek support from **licensed mental health professionals**, such as psychologists, psychiatrists, therapists, or counselors, as well as **qualified financial professionals**, including financial planners, accountants, or credit counselors, when appropriate. If you are experiencing severe emotional distress, financial crisis, thoughts of self-harm, or an inability to function in daily life, please seek **immediate professional or emergency assistance**.

The content of this book is based on **general knowledge, lived experience, trauma-informed perspectives, and educational research**, and is meant to foster awareness, validation, and self-reflection. Individual experiences with money, trauma, and stress vary widely. What resonates with one reader may not apply to another.

Any exercises, reflections, prompts, or conceptual frameworks included in this book are **voluntary and self-directed**. Readers assume full responsibility for how they interpret and apply the material. The author and publisher make no guarantees regarding financial outcomes, emotional results, or personal transformation.

This book does not encourage reckless financial behavior, avoidance of professional care, or replacement of evidence-based treatment. It is designed to **complement**, not replace, responsible support systems and professional guidance.

By reading this book, you acknowledge that you understand and accept that:

- You are responsible for your own mental, emotional, and financial decisions
- This book is not professional advice
- Healing and recovery are non-linear and deeply personal processes

The author writes with empathy and care, recognizing that financial trauma can be deeply intertwined with shame, fear, survival, and identity. This book is offered as a **compassionate resource**, not a cure, diagnosis, or promise.

Introduction

Every email from your bank shouldn't feel like a bomb.

Yet for many people, it does.

A subject line flashes across your screen—*payment due*, *account alert*, *balance update*—and suddenly your body reacts before your mind can catch up. Your chest tightens. Your stomach drops. Your thoughts scatter. You haven't even opened the message, but your nervous system has already decided: *danger*.

This book begins there.

Not with numbers, budgets, or spreadsheets—but with the **moment your heart starts racing**, the moment your hands feel cold, the moment your brain jumps years into the future or snaps back to the past. Because for many people, money is no longer just money. It has become a trigger.

If every bill feels like a threat...
If payday brings dread instead of relief...
If you freeze, avoid, obsess, or spiral when finances come up...

This may be more than "bad money habits" or "not trying hard enough."
It may be **financial trauma replaying itself in real time**.

This book uses the term *Money PTSD* not as a clinical label, but as a way to name a lived experience: what happens when **past financial harm hijacks the present**. When eviction notices, shut-off warnings, overdraft fees, debt collectors, unstable income, medical bills, or long periods of scarcity teach your nervous system that survival is always on the line.

Trauma doesn't disappear just because circumstances change.
It rewires how you perceive risk, safety, time, and control.

So even when things are "okay" on paper, your body may still be bracing for collapse.

You might:

- Check your bank balance compulsively—or avoid it entirely
- Feel shame or panic when spending even small amounts
- Experience mental fog, dissociation, or anger around money
- Relive past financial disasters every single month
- Feel like you're always one step from losing everything

This book is not here to judge that response.

It's here to explain it.

Money PTSD is not about being irresponsible. It is about **having learned—through real experience—that money problems hurt deeply and unpredictably**. That they can cost you housing, dignity, safety, relationships, health, or peace of mind. Your system adapted to survive that reality. The problem is that survival wiring doesn't turn itself off automatically.

So every payday becomes a checkpoint.
Every bill becomes a flashback.
Every unexpected expense becomes a reminder of how fast things once fell apart.

This book is a roadmap for **stopping those replays**.

Not by pretending money isn't stressful.
Not by shaming yourself into discipline.
Not by bypassing fear with forced positivity.

But by understanding:

- How trauma lives in the body, not just the mind
- Why logic fails when the nervous system is activated
- How financial stress collapses time into constant emergency
- Why "just budgeting better" often makes things worse
- How to gently rewire safety without denying reality

This is about reclaiming **peace**, not perfection.

You do not need to become wealthy to heal.
You do not need to be debt-free to calm your body.
You do not need to "fix everything" to stop feeling hunted by money.

What you need is a new relationship with threat, time, and self-trust.

This book will help you recognize when the alarm you feel is coming from *now*—and when it's coming from *then*. It will help you separate today's numbers from yesterday's wounds. It will give language to experiences you may have never been able to explain, and permission to stop blaming yourself for reactions that were learned under pressure.

If your heart races at every bill, this book is for you.
If payday feels like a trial instead of a relief, this book is for you.
If money has become a source of fear rather than a tool, this book is for you.

You are not broken.
Your nervous system is exhausted.

And this book is the beginning of teaching it that the danger has changed—and that peace is possible again.

Chapter 1: Defining Financial PTSD

What Financial PTSD Really Is

Financial PTSD is not about being "bad with money." It is what happens when repeated or severe financial stress teaches your nervous system that money equals danger. Over time, your body learns to respond to financial cues—bills, balances, paydays, bank notifications—as if they are threats to survival. This response is automatic, fast, and often overwhelming.

Unlike ordinary stress, financial trauma does not fade when the immediate crisis ends. Even after income stabilizes or debts shrink, the body may still react as though catastrophe is imminent. This is because trauma is stored in the nervous system, not in spreadsheets. Your system remembers what it cost you before—sleep, housing, health, dignity—and it prepares to prevent that pain from happening again.

Financial PTSD often develops slowly. Years of scarcity, instability, medical expenses, unemployment, exploitation, or sudden loss can accumulate until the body stops trusting money altogether. Each new financial interaction becomes a reminder of how quickly things once fell apart.

This is why logic alone rarely works. You can *know* you're okay and still feel panic. You can *see* the numbers and still feel chased. Financial PTSD lives in reflexes, not reasoning.

Naming this experience matters. When you understand that your reactions are trauma-based adaptations, shame loosens its grip. You are not weak—you are responding exactly as a system trained under threat would respond.

How Financial Trauma Hijacks the Nervous System

The nervous system's primary job is survival. When money becomes linked to danger, the system rewires itself to stay alert. This is why even neutral financial events can trigger fight, flight, freeze, or collapse responses.

Fight may look like anger at bills, impulsive spending, or hostility around money conversations. Flight often shows up as avoidance—unopened mail, ignored accounts, delayed decisions. Freeze can appear as paralysis, brain fog, or inability to act even when you want to. Collapse may look like numbness, hopelessness, or giving up entirely.

These reactions are not character flaws. They are biological responses learned during moments when money truly threatened safety. The body does not distinguish between past and present threats—it reacts to patterns.

Financial trauma also distorts time. The nervous system pulls the past into the present, making every bill feel like the one that once destroyed stability. This is why reactions often feel disproportionate to the actual situation.

Understanding this mechanism is the first step toward healing. You cannot calm a system you are constantly blaming. Regulation begins with recognition.

Why Financial PTSD Is Often Misdiagnosed as Anxiety

Many people with financial PTSD are told they "just have anxiety." While anxiety may be present, it does not fully explain the depth and specificity of the response to money-related triggers.

General anxiety tends to be diffuse. Financial PTSD is targeted. The body may feel calm until money enters the picture—then the alarm activates instantly. This pattern is a hallmark of trauma.

Another key difference is memory. Financial PTSD carries emotional and somatic memories tied to real past harm. The fear is not hypothetical—it is remembered. The body is responding to history, not imagination.

When this distinction is missed, people are often given surface-level solutions: budget harder, think positive, be disciplined. These approaches can unintentionally retraumatize, reinforcing the belief that something is wrong with you.

Proper framing shifts the goal. Instead of forcing control, the work becomes restoring safety and trust—internally first, financially second.

Common Signs You May Be Experiencing Financial PTSD

One of the clearest signs is disproportionate reaction. A small expense triggers a massive emotional response. A routine bill feels catastrophic. The intensity does not match the moment—it matches the memory.

Another sign is avoidance paired with obsession. You may avoid checking finances for weeks, then obsessively check multiple times a day. This oscillation reflects a system torn between fear and hypervigilance.

Physical symptoms are common: racing heart, nausea, dizziness, muscle tension, shallow breathing. These are not "overreactions"—they are stress responses activated by perceived threat.

Shame is also a major indicator. Financial PTSD often comes with harsh self-talk, secrecy, and isolation. Many people feel they must hide their financial reality to stay safe socially or emotionally.

Recognizing these patterns allows you to shift from self-judgment to self-observation. Awareness creates space for change.

How Financial PTSD Affects Decision-Making

Trauma narrows perception. When the nervous system is activated, the brain prioritizes short-term survival over long-term planning. This is why people with financial PTSD may struggle with decisions even when they understand the math.

Scarcity thinking takes over. The future feels compressed. Everything feels urgent. This can lead to impulsive choices or total indecision—both are attempts to escape discomfort.

Financial PTSD also erodes trust in self. Past losses can convince you that you always choose wrong, making every decision feel dangerous. Over time, confidence collapses.

This is not a lack of intelligence or willpower. It is a predictable outcome of stress chemistry interfering with executive function.

Healing restores choice. As the nervous system calms, clarity returns—not because you forced it, but because safety allowed it.

Why Defining Financial PTSD Is an Act of Power

Language shapes experience. When you name financial PTSD, you stop internalizing a system failure as a personal defect. You reclaim authorship of your story.

Definition creates boundaries. It separates your identity from your symptoms. You are not "bad with money"—you are healing from harm.

This naming also opens doors to compassion. Toward yourself. Toward others. Toward the parts of you that adapted under pressure.

Financial PTSD is not permanent. Nervous systems are plastic. They can relearn safety with patience and consistency.

This chapter is not about diagnosis. It is about validation—and validation is often the first moment of relief.

Financial Tip: Stabilize Before You Strategize

Before trying to "fix" your finances, prioritize nervous system stabilization. Calm bodies make better decisions than panicked ones. This may mean slowing down instead of rushing to optimize.

Create a simple ritual around financial tasks: same time, same place, limited duration. Predictability reduces threat. Your body needs to know the encounter has an end.

Progress is measured in reduced panic, not perfect plans. If you feel calmer after engaging with money—even briefly—that is success.

Exercise 1: Identifying Your Money Triggers
Steps:

1. Write down the last three times money caused a strong emotional reaction.
2. Note what specifically triggered it (email, bill, conversation, thought).
3. Describe the physical sensations you felt in your body.
4. Identify whether the reaction felt tied to a past memory or fear.

This exercise builds awareness without judgment. You are mapping patterns, not fixing them yet.

Exercise 2: Separating Past From Present
Steps:

1. Choose one current financial stressor.
2. Write what is objectively happening now.
3. Write what your body fears will happen.
4. Ask: "Has this already happened before?"
5. Gently label what belongs to the past versus the present.

This helps your nervous system distinguish memory from reality.

Exercise 3: Creating a Safety Anchor
Steps:

1. Choose a physical action (breathing, grounding touch, posture).
2. Practice it daily when calm.
3. Use it intentionally before engaging with money.
4. Repeat until your body associates money with regulation instead of panic.

Consistency matters more than intensity.

Financial Idea 1: Trauma-Informed Budgeting

Traditional budgets focus on restriction. Trauma-informed budgeting focuses on predictability and safety. The goal is not control—it is trust.

Start with fixed, known expenses only. Avoid micromanaging variable categories at first. Stability builds tolerance.

Over time, flexibility can be introduced. Healing happens in layers.

Financial Idea 2: The Minimum Viable Financial System

Instead of optimizing everything, build the smallest system that works. One account. One tracking method. One review day.

Complexity increases stress. Simplicity creates capacity.

As safety increases, systems can grow—but only when the body is ready.

Financial Idea 3: Money as Information, Not Judgment

Shift your mindset: numbers are data, not moral verdicts. They describe, they do not accuse.

Practice observing balances without interpreting them as success or failure.

Neutral observation is a powerful step toward healing.

Journal Prompts

1. What money-related event taught me fear the first time?
2. How does my body react to financial stress before my mind does?
3. What do I fear money will take from me?
4. What does financial safety feel like in my body?
5. When do I feel most calm around money?
6. What messages about money did I absorb growing up?
7. How do I punish myself financially without realizing it?
8. What would gentleness with money look like?
9. What part of me learned to survive financial chaos?
10. What would it mean to trust myself again?

Closing Reflection

Defining financial PTSD is not about labeling yourself—it is about freeing yourself. When you understand that your reactions were learned under pressure, blame softens into compassion. This chapter is the foundation. From here, healing becomes possible—not by forcing change, but by restoring safety, one moment at a time.

Chapter 2: Symptoms You May Not Know Are Trauma

Before diving deeper, it's important to name what often goes unnoticed. Many people living with financial trauma believe their reactions are personality flaws, laziness, or irresponsibility. In reality, these are **trauma responses**—learned survival patterns that once protected you.

Symptoms That Are Often Misread or Missed

1. **Bank Account Avoidance** — You delay checking balances because your body anticipates danger before your mind does.
2. **Payday Dread** — Income days trigger anxiety instead of relief due to past cycles of loss.
3. **Impulse Spending After Stress** — Spending becomes a nervous system discharge, not a financial decision.
4. **Financial Paralysis** — You know what to do but feel physically unable to act.
5. **Shame Spirals** — One expense triggers harsh self-judgment and emotional collapse.
6. **Over-Explaining Purchases** — You feel compelled to justify spending to others—or yourself.
7. **Catastrophic Thinking** — Small expenses feel like the beginning of total ruin.
8. **Obsessive Balance Checking** — Hypervigilance replaces trust and creates constant stress.
9. **Emotional Numbness Around Money** — Detachment becomes a defense against overwhelm.
10. **Irritability During Money Conversations** — Your nervous system interprets discussion as threat.
11. **Difficulty Planning Long-Term** — Trauma collapses time into constant short-term survival.

12. **Fear of Asking for Help** — Past consequences taught you that needing support is dangerous.
13. **Physical Symptoms During Financial Tasks** — Headaches, nausea, tight chest, or dizziness appear.
14. **All-or-Nothing Money Thinking** — You swing between extreme control and total avoidance.
15. **Feeling "Bad" No Matter What You Do** — Even responsible actions don't register as safety.

Why Trauma Symptoms Don't Look Like Trauma

When people imagine trauma, they often picture dramatic events. Financial trauma is quieter. It hides in routines, emails, and calendar reminders. Because money stress is normalized, its traumatic impact is rarely recognized.

These symptoms develop gradually. Each bill paid under fear, each month survived under pressure, each moment of uncertainty trains the nervous system to stay alert. Over time, hypervigilance feels normal.

Society often reinforces this invisibility. Struggle is framed as personal failure rather than systemic harm or accumulated stress. This framing deepens shame and keeps trauma unnamed.

Because symptoms don't match stereotypes, people push themselves harder instead of seeking gentleness. This worsens the cycle.

Recognizing these signs as trauma responses interrupts that loop.

How the Body Carries Financial Trauma

The body remembers what the mind tries to forget. Financial trauma is stored somatically—in muscle tension, breath patterns, posture, and stress chemistry.

Money-related cues activate the same physiological responses as physical threats. Cortisol rises. Heart rate increases. Digestion slows. Thinking narrows.

This is why you may feel "out of control" even when nothing is happening. The body is responding to conditioned memory, not present danger.

Trying to reason your way out rarely works. Regulation must happen at the body level first.

When the body feels safer, the mind follows.

Emotional Responses That Are Actually Survival Strategies

Anger around money often masks fear. Avoidance protects against overwhelm. Numbness prevents emotional flooding. These are not failures—they are adaptations.

Each response once served a purpose. They helped you get through moments when resources were scarce or consequences were severe.

Problems arise when these strategies persist beyond the crisis. What once protected you now limits you.

Healing does not require eliminating these responses. It requires updating them.

Respecting their origin allows them to soften.

Why Symptoms Intensify Even When Finances Improve

One of the most confusing aspects of financial trauma is escalation during stability. As pressure eases, stored fear surfaces.

Safety gives the nervous system room to process what it couldn't before. Symptoms intensify not because things are worse—but because your system finally has capacity.

This is often misinterpreted as failure or regression. In reality, it's delayed processing.

Understanding this prevents panic and self-blame.

Stability doesn't erase trauma—it reveals it.

The Cost of Ignoring These Symptoms

Unaddressed financial trauma compounds over time. Decision fatigue increases. Relationships strain. Health deteriorates.

Ignoring symptoms forces the nervous system to work harder to maintain control. Burnout follows.

Patterns repeat not because you want them to—but because they're unexamined.

Naming symptoms creates choice. Choice restores agency.

Awareness is not weakness. It is intervention.

What Changes When Symptoms Are Named

Language brings relief. When symptoms are named as trauma responses, shame loosens.

You stop fighting yourself. You start working with your system instead of against it.

This shift alone can reduce intensity. The body no longer has to scream to be heard.

From here, healing becomes collaborative.

You are no longer the problem. The pattern is.

Financial Tip: Track Reactions, Not Just Numbers

Instead of focusing only on expenses, track emotional responses. Notice when tension spikes, when avoidance appears, when relief fades quickly.

This builds self-awareness without pressure to change behavior immediately.

Understanding reactions is the foundation of sustainable financial healing.

Exercise 1: Symptom Mapping
Steps:

1. Review the symptom list above.
2. Circle the ones you recognize.
3. Note when they first appeared in your life.
4. Write what was happening financially at that time.

Patterns often reveal origin points.

Exercise 2: Body Check During Money Tasks
Steps:

1. Choose one small financial task.
2. Pause before starting and scan your body.
3. Name sensations without judgment.
4. Breathe until intensity drops slightly.
5. Complete the task slowly.

This retrains safety.

Exercise 3: Reframing the Symptom
Steps:

1. Pick one symptom you dislike.
2. Write how it once protected you.
3. Thank it for its role.
4. Ask what support it needs now.

Compassion changes patterns faster than force.

Financial Idea 1: Reaction-Based Budgeting

Instead of budgeting by category alone, budget by stress level. Identify which expenses trigger the most fear.

Address those gently first. Safety before optimization.

This reduces emotional overload.

Financial Idea 2: Limiting Financial Exposure Windows

Set specific times for financial engagement. Outside those windows, disengage.

This reduces chronic activation.

Boundaries create relief.

Financial Idea 3: Externalizing the Numbers

View finances as an external system—not a reflection of worth.

Use neutral language: "The account shows" instead of "I failed."

Language rewires perception.

Journal Prompts

1. Which money symptoms surprise me the most?
2. How has my body protected me financially?
3. What symptom do I judge myself for unfairly?
4. When do I feel safest with money?
5. How does fear show up in my spending?
6. What does avoidance protect me from?
7. What would financial gentleness look like?
8. How has shame shaped my money habits?
9. What does my nervous system need to feel safer?
10. What would change if I trusted myself more?

Closing Reflection

Many of the behaviors you've been taught to fix are actually signals asking to be understood. When symptoms are recognized as trauma responses, self-attack gives way to curiosity. This chapter is not about labeling yourself—it's about reclaiming compassion. Healing begins when you stop asking, "What's wrong with me?" and start asking, "What happened to me—and how can I support myself now?"

Chapter 3: What Triggers Your Nervous System Today

Trauma does not live in the past—it activates in the present. Your nervous system is not reacting to numbers on a screen; it is responding to **signals it has learned to associate with threat**. Many of today's triggers look ordinary on the surface, which is why they often go unnoticed and untreated.

Common Financial Triggers Your Body Still Responds To

1. **Bank Notifications** — Automated alerts activate danger before you read the message.
2. **Bills With Due Dates** — Time pressure signals urgency and loss of control.
3. **Unexpected Expenses** — Surprise costs echo past instability.
4. **Low Account Balances** — Numbers trigger survival fear regardless of context.
5. **Debt Statements** — Seeing totals reactivates shame and overwhelm.
6. **Payday Cycles** — Income reminds the body of past boom-and-bust patterns.
7. **Money Conversations** — Discussion feels like exposure or judgment.
8. **Asking for Help** — Support requests recall punishment or rejection.
9. **Spending on Yourself** — Self-care conflicts with survival conditioning.
10. **Financial Planning** — Future focus feels unsafe when the past collapsed suddenly.
11. **Opening Mail** — Paper reminders carry emotional weight.
12. **Account Logins** — Passwords precede anticipated bad news.
13. **Price Increases** — Rising costs activate scarcity memory.
14. **Comparing Finances** — Social comparison triggers inadequacy and threat.

15. **Silence From Institutions** — No news feels as dangerous as bad news.

Why Triggers Are About Meaning, Not Money

Triggers are not logical. They are symbolic. Your nervous system responds to what money *meant* during moments of danger, not what it objectively means now.

For some, money meant eviction. For others, it meant medical crises, abandonment, or loss of dignity. The body remembers consequences, not calculations.

This is why a harmless notification can feel like a punch to the chest. The trigger is not the message—it is the memory it activates.

Triggers operate faster than conscious thought. By the time you rationalize, the body has already reacted.

Healing requires decoding meaning, not eliminating money.

How the Nervous System Detects Threat Today

The nervous system scans for familiar patterns. When it detects similarities to past danger, it activates immediately.

Triggers often involve **uncertainty, urgency, visibility, or lack of control**—the same elements present during earlier financial trauma.

Modern systems amplify this response. Apps, alerts, deadlines, and automation increase exposure frequency.

The result is chronic activation rather than isolated stress.

Recognizing this pattern explains why exhaustion persists even when crises end.

Why Some Triggers Feel Irrational

Trauma does not follow logic. A small expense can trigger more panic than a large planned one because surprise equals danger.

Predictability calms the nervous system. Ambiguity activates it.

You may feel ashamed for reacting "too strongly." That shame compounds the response.

The truth is your nervous system is responding exactly as it was trained to.

Rational understanding comes later—regulation comes first.

Triggers Are Invitations, Not Failures

Each trigger points to a wound asking for safety, not discipline.

Instead of asking, "Why can't I handle this?" ask, "What does this remind my body of?"

Triggers are information. They show where trust was broken.

They also show where healing is possible.

Listening reduces intensity.

How Awareness Changes the Response

Naming a trigger slows the reaction. The body feels seen.

When you can say, "This is a trigger," you create distance between stimulus and response.

That space allows choice.

Choice restores agency.

Agency rebuilds trust.

Financial Tip: Reduce Surprise Wherever Possible

Surprise is a primary trigger. Automate predictable expenses, calendar reminders, and review times.

Knowing *when* you'll engage with money reduces nervous system load.

Predictability is a form of safety.

Exercise 1: Trigger Identification Map
Steps:

1. Review the trigger list.
2. Highlight the top five that activate you.
3. Write what each trigger reminds your body of.
4. Note physical sensations associated with each.

This reveals emotional memory.

Exercise 2: Trigger Response Pause
Steps:

1. When triggered, stop before acting.
2. Name the trigger out loud or in writing.
3. Ground your body (breath, touch, posture).
4. Delay response by 10 minutes.

Pause restores regulation.

Exercise 3: Safety Reassignment
Steps:

1. Choose one frequent trigger.
2. Pair it with a calming ritual.
3. Repeat consistently.
4. Allow your nervous system to relearn association.

Repetition rewires threat.

Financial Idea 1: Trigger-Aware Scheduling
Plan financial tasks around energy, not deadlines alone.
Avoid engaging when exhausted or overwhelmed.
Timing matters more than effort.

Financial Idea 2: De-Weaponizing Notifications
Turn off nonessential alerts. Choose when information reaches you.
Control exposure to reduce activation.
You decide when money enters your nervous system.

Financial Idea 3: Emotional Cost Accounting
Consider emotional cost alongside financial cost.
Sometimes peace is worth more than optimization.
Trauma-informed decisions protect long-term capacity.

Journal Prompts

1. Which triggers surprise me most?
2. What do my strongest triggers remind me of?
3. How does my body signal threat?
4. What reduces intensity fastest?
5. Where do I feel safest with money?
6. How does surprise affect me financially?
7. What financial task feels least threatening?
8. How can I add predictability?
9. What would safety look like today?
10. What trigger am I ready to soften?

Closing Reflection

Triggers are not proof that you are failing—they are proof that your nervous system remembers. When you learn what activates you, you stop being blindsided by your own reactions. This chapter is not about eliminating triggers; it is about understanding them. Awareness turns threat into information, and information restores power. From here, peace becomes something you can practice—not something you wait for.

Chapter 4: Interrupting Flashbacks and Fear Spirals

What a Financial Flashback Actually Is

A financial flashback is not remembering a past event—it is *reliving* it in the body. When a bill, balance, or conversation activates you, your nervous system reacts as if the original threat is happening again. Time collapses. The present moment disappears.

Unlike visual flashbacks often portrayed in media, financial flashbacks are usually emotional and physical. Your chest tightens. Your breath shortens. Your thoughts race or shut down. You may feel small, trapped, or desperate without knowing why.

These flashbacks are fueled by memory stored outside conscious awareness. The body remembers what the mind may not clearly recall. This is why reassurance rarely works in the moment—logic cannot override survival chemistry.

Fear spirals often follow. One thought triggers another: *What if I can't pay this? What if it gets worse? What if everything falls apart again?* The spiral accelerates until the nervous system is overwhelmed.

Understanding that this is a flashback—not a prediction—creates the first interruption.

How Fear Spirals Gain Momentum

Fear spirals thrive on speed. Once activated, the nervous system pushes the mind to scan for more danger. Thoughts stack rapidly, each one escalating the threat.

Money-related spirals often move from a single expense to imagined total collapse. The brain leaps forward in time, bypassing nuance and probability.

This happens because trauma prioritizes certainty over accuracy. The worst-case scenario feels safer than uncertainty, even if it's painful.

As the spiral intensifies, the body tightens further. Breathing becomes shallow. Muscles brace. Digestion halts. Decision-making shuts down.

Interrupting the spiral requires slowing—not solving.

Why You Can't Think Your Way Out

When fear is active, the brain regions responsible for reasoning and planning go offline. This is not a failure—it is a biological response.

Trying to force logic during a flashback often backfires. The body interprets pressure as additional threat.

This is why people feel frustrated with themselves for "knowing better" but still panicking. Knowledge does not equal regulation.

The sequence matters: body first, mind second.

When the nervous system calms, clarity returns naturally.

Grounding the Body to Exit the Past

Grounding brings attention back to the present moment. It reminds the nervous system that the danger is not happening *now*.

Simple physical cues—feet on the floor, temperature awareness, steady breathing—anchor you in current reality.

Grounding does not deny fear. It reassures the body that it is safe enough to stand down.

Repetition is key. One grounding attempt may only reduce intensity slightly—and that is enough.

Progress is measured in interruption, not elimination.

Rewriting the Spiral Pathway

Each time you interrupt a flashback, you weaken the old pathway and strengthen a new one.

Neuroplasticity means your nervous system can learn alternatives to panic.

This learning happens through experience, not insight alone.

Consistency matters more than perfection.

Every interruption is a vote for peace.

Building Trust Through Repetition

Trust is rebuilt through predictable response. When your system learns that fear will be met with care—not criticism—it softens.

Over time, triggers lose intensity. Spirals shorten. Recovery speeds up.

This does not mean fear disappears. It means fear no longer controls you.

You are teaching your nervous system a new outcome.

That is healing in motion.

Financial Tip: Pause Spending During Activation

Do not make financial decisions while activated. Fear-driven choices often create regret.

Create a personal rule: no purchases or major decisions until your body settles.

This protects both your finances and your nervous system.

Exercise 1: The Flashback Interrupt
Steps:

1. Notice the first signs of activation.
2. Say internally: "This is a memory, not a prediction."
3. Place your feet firmly on the floor.
4. Take five slow breaths, counting each exhale.
5. Name three things you can see.

This brings you back to now.

Exercise 2: Spiral Slowing Script
Steps:

1. Write down the spiraling thoughts as they appear.
2. Circle the first thought that started it.
3. Gently remind yourself: “I don’t have to solve this right now.”
4. Delay problem-solving for 30 minutes.

Delay interrupts escalation.

Exercise 3: Post-Trigger Care
Steps:

1. After a flashback, do something regulating.
2. Avoid self-criticism.
3. Note what helped reduce intensity.
4. Repeat what worked next time.

Recovery reinforces safety.

Financial Idea 1: The 24-Hour Rule

Major financial actions wait 24 hours after emotional activation.

This protects against trauma-driven urgency.

Time restores perspective.

Financial Idea 2: Prewritten Reassurance Statements

Create statements you read during fear: “I have survived before. This moment will pass.”

Prepared language reduces cognitive load.

Familiar words calm faster.

Financial Idea 3: Separating Review From Action

Review finances without acting. Action can come later.

This trains tolerance without pressure.

Gradual exposure builds confidence.

Journal Prompts

1. How does a financial flashback feel in my body?
2. What thoughts usually start my spirals?
3. What helps me return to the present fastest?
4. How do I treat myself during fear?
5. What would gentleness look like mid-spiral?
6. What has fear protected me from?
7. How long do spirals usually last?
8. What shortens them?
9. How can I prepare for future triggers?
10. What would trust feel like in my body?

Closing Reflection

Fear spirals are not failures—they are memories asking to be interrupted. Each time you slow, ground, and care for yourself during activation, you reclaim time from the past. This chapter is about learning that fear does not need to be defeated to be softened. It needs to be met, steadied, and reminded that you are here, now, and no longer alone with it.

Chapter 5: Creating New Money Memories Safely

Why Healing Requires New Experiences, Not Just Insight

Understanding financial trauma is powerful, but insight alone does not rewire the nervous system. Trauma is learned through experience, and it is healed the same way—through *new experiences that contradict old expectations*. Your body does not change because it understands; it changes because it *feels* something different.

If your past taught you that money leads to danger, loss, or shame, your system is still operating under that rule. Even when finances improve, the rule remains unless it is gently challenged. Healing happens when your nervous system encounters money and nothing bad happens.

This is why "doing everything right" and still feeling afraid is so common. You have not yet created enough *safe money memories* to outweigh the painful ones. The body needs repetition, not reassurance.

Creating new money memories does not mean taking risks or forcing confidence. It means **small, predictable interactions with money that end in safety**. The goal is not excitement or success—it is neutrality.

Safety is what teaches the nervous system that the rules have changed.

What a Safe Money Memory Looks Like

A safe money memory is simple and often quiet. It might be paying a bill and noticing it did not lead to catastrophe. It might be checking your balance and realizing you survived the discomfort. It might be spending a small amount and feeling okay afterward.

These moments often feel insignificant to the logical mind, but they are enormous to a traumatized nervous system. Each one is evidence that money interaction does not always equal harm.

Safe money memories are not about winning. They are about *ending the interaction regulated*. Calm completion matters more than outcomes.

Importantly, safety does not mean the absence of stress. It means stress that resolves instead of spirals. It means returning to baseline.

When these moments accumulate, your system begins to expect safety instead of threat.

Why Rushing Recreates Trauma

One of the most common mistakes in financial healing is rushing. Pushing yourself to "get over it," take bigger steps, or face everything at once often recreates the original trauma dynamics.

Trauma was overwhelming, fast, and out of your control. Healing must be the opposite: **slow, chosen, and contained**. If your body feels flooded, you are not healing—you are reliving.

Progress that feels unbearable is not progress. It teaches your nervous system that money is still unsafe.

Going slowly is not avoidance. It is precision.

The pace of healing is set by your nervous system, not your goals.

Rebuilding Trust With Yourself First

Before trusting money, you must trust *yourself* with money. Trauma often breaks self-trust by teaching you that your decisions lead to pain.

Each safe money memory repairs this trust. When you engage with money and respond kindly to yourself—regardless of outcome—you prove that you can handle discomfort without collapse.

Self-trust grows when you stop abandoning yourself during stress. Staying present, grounding, and refusing self-attack are acts of repair.

This is why emotional safety matters more than financial perfection. You can rebuild money stability later; nervous system safety comes first.

When you trust yourself, money loses its power to threaten your identity.

Using Neutrality to Replace Fear

The goal of this chapter is not to make money feel good. That may come later. Right now, neutrality is enough.

Neutral experiences teach the nervous system that money does not always require emotional energy. Calm, boring interactions are healing.

This is why repetitive, low-stakes actions are so effective. They normalize money instead of dramatizing it.

Over time, neutrality creates space. Space allows curiosity. Curiosity allows growth.

Peace is built from ordinary moments repeated consistently.

How New Memories Override Old Ones

The nervous system updates through contrast. When new experiences consistently contradict old expectations, the system revises its rules.

This does not erase the past. It simply stops letting the past control the present.

Old memories lose intensity when they are no longer reinforced. New ones gain strength through repetition.

This process takes time, patience, and compassion.

Every safe interaction is a vote for the future you are building.

Financial Tip: Start With Predictable Wins

Choose financial actions with high predictability and low risk. Pay the same bill, at the same time, in the same way.

Consistency builds safety faster than variety.

Let your nervous system learn what to expect.

Exercise 1: The Safe Money Interaction
Steps:

1. Choose one small financial task you can complete easily.
2. Do it slowly and intentionally.
3. Ground your body before and after.
4. Notice that nothing bad happened.
5. Write one sentence about how it felt afterward.

This creates a recorded safe memory.

Exercise 2: Neutral Exposure Practice
Steps:

1. Set a timer for five minutes.
2. Open your banking app or financial document.
3. Observe without making changes.
4. Close it when the timer ends.
5. Regulate your body afterward.

Exposure without pressure builds tolerance.

Exercise 3: Repairing After Discomfort
Steps:

1. After a stressful money interaction, pause.
2. Name one thing you handled well.
3. Offer yourself reassurance instead of critique.
4. Engage in a calming activity.

Repair prevents retraumatization.

Financial Idea 1: Repetition Over Optimization

Do the same simple actions repeatedly rather than chasing efficiency.

Familiarity calms the nervous system.

Optimization can wait.

Financial Idea 2: Emotional Safety Budgeting

Budget emotional capacity alongside money. Limit how many financial tasks you do at once.

Energy is a resource.

Protect it.

Financial Idea 3: Celebrating Completion, Not Outcome

Celebrate finishing tasks, not results.

Completion teaches safety.

Outcomes come later.

Journal Prompts

1. What money interactions feel safest right now?
2. When have I handled money without disaster?
3. What pace feels supportive to my body?
4. How do I treat myself after financial stress?
5. What does neutrality feel like?
6. What would gentler progress look like?
7. Where do I rush myself unnecessarily?
8. How can I build predictability?
9. What does self-trust mean to me?
10. What new money memory do I want to create next?

Closing Reflection

Healing financial trauma is not about rewriting the past—it is about giving your nervous system new evidence. Each safe interaction with money tells a different story: that you can engage, feel discomfort, and still be okay. These moments may feel small, but they are the foundation of peace. Over time, new memories soften old ones, and money becomes what it was always meant to be—a tool, not a threat.

Appendix A: Four Grounding Techniques for Panic-Free Banking

This appendix is designed to be **practical, immediate, and repeatable**. These grounding techniques are not about forcing calm or eliminating fear. They are about **keeping your nervous system anchored in the present** while engaging with money.

You do not need to master all four. One effective technique used consistently is more powerful than many used occasionally. Choose what fits your body, not what sounds best on paper.

Use these techniques **before, during, or after** banking tasks such as checking balances, paying bills, reviewing statements, or opening financial emails.

Grounding Technique 1: The Five-Minute Financial Container

Purpose:
To prevent panic by giving your nervous system a clear beginning and end to financial engagement.

Trauma reacts strongly to open-ended exposure. When your body doesn't know how long the threat will last, it stays hyper-alert. This technique creates **predictable limits**, which signal safety.

How to Practice:

1. Set a timer for **five minutes** before opening any banking app or document.
2. Say to yourself (out loud if possible): *"I will stop when the timer ends."*
3. Engage only with the specific task you chose—nothing extra.
4. When the timer ends, **stop immediately**, even if you feel unfinished.
5. Close the app or document and physically move away from it.

Why It Works:
Your nervous system learns that money engagement is **contained and survivable**. Over time, panic decreases because your body trusts the boundary.

When to Use:

- Checking balances
- Reviewing transactions
- Opening statements
- Paying routine bills

Grounding Technique 2: The Body Anchor Before Login

Purpose:

To bring your body into the present moment before money activates fear memory.

Financial panic often begins *before* the task starts. This technique anchors you **physically**, so your body doesn't slip into past threat.

How to Practice:

1. Before logging in, place both feet firmly on the floor.
2. Press your toes gently downward and notice the pressure.
3. Place one hand on your chest or stomach.
4. Take **five slow exhales** (longer out-breath than in-breath).
5. Name silently: *"I am here. This is now."*

Only after completing this do you proceed with banking.

Why It Works:

Trauma pulls awareness into the past. Physical sensation pulls it back to now. The body cannot be in two times at once.

When to Use:

- Logging into banking apps
- Opening financial emails
- Starting any money-related task

Grounding Technique 3: Sensory Reality Check During Banking

Purpose:

To interrupt panic mid-task by reminding your nervous system of current safety.

When fear spikes during banking, grounding must be **immediate and sensory**. This technique reorients your system without stopping the task entirely.

How to Practice:

1. Pause what you are doing without closing the app.
2. Name **three things you can see** in the room.
3. Name **two things you can feel** physically (chair, floor, clothing).
4. Name **one thing you can hear** right now.
5. Take one slow breath before continuing or stopping.

Why It Works:

Panic collapses awareness inward. Sensory grounding expands it outward. This shift reduces intensity without requiring explanation or reassurance.

When to Use:

- Mid-panic while reviewing balances
- During fear spirals
- When your body starts reacting strongly

Grounding Technique 4: Post-Banking Nervous System Reset

Purpose:

To prevent lingering anxiety after financial tasks.

Many people finish banking tasks but stay activated for hours. This technique teaches your nervous system that **the task is over** and it can stand down.

How to Practice:

1. After completing the task, stand up or change rooms.
2. Stretch or shake your arms and hands for 30 seconds.
3. Take three deep breaths while looking around the room.
4. Say internally: *"The money task is finished."*
5. Engage in a neutral or pleasant activity for at least five minutes.

Why It Works:

Trauma systems often don't recognize completion. This ritual marks an **end point**, which reduces residual anxiety and future avoidance.

When to Use:

- After paying bills
- After reviewing finances
- After any stressful money interaction

How to Choose the Right Technique

- If panic starts **before** you begin → Use Technique 2
- If panic rises **during** the task → Use Technique 3
- If panic lingers **after** the task → Use Technique 4
- If money feels overwhelming overall → Use Technique 1

You may combine techniques as needed.

Practice Notes

- These techniques work through **repetition**, not force
- Mild reduction in panic is success
- You are teaching safety, not demanding calm
- Consistency matters more than intensity

If one technique doesn't work, it doesn't mean you failed—it means your nervous system prefers a different language.

Closing Note for Appendix A

Panic-free banking does not mean fear disappears. It means fear no longer controls your actions. These grounding techniques are tools for reclaiming agency, one interaction at a time. Each time you use them, you are telling your nervous system: *"We can engage with money and remain safe."* Over time, that message becomes belief.

Message from the Author:

I hope you enjoyed this book, I love astrology and knew there was not a book such as this out on the shelf. I love metaphysical items as well. Please check out my other books:

-Life of Government Benefits

-My life of Hell

-My life with Hydrocephalus

-Red Sky

-World Domination:Woman's rule

-World Domination:Woman's Rule 2: The War

-Life and Banishment of Apophis: book 1

-The Kidney Friendly Diet

-The Ultimate Hemp Cookbook

-Creating a Dispensary(legally)

-Cleanliness throughout life: the importance of showering from childhood to adulthood.

-Strong Roots: The Risks of Overcoddling children

-Hemp Horoscopes: Cosmic Insights and Earthly Healing

- Celestial Hemp Navigating the Zodiac: Through the Green Cosmos

-Astrological Hemp: Aligning The Stars with Earth's Ancient Herb

-The Astrological Guide to Hemp: Stars, Signs, and Sacred Leaves

-Green Growth: Innovative Marketing Strategies for your Hemp Products and Dispensary

-Cosmic Cannabis

-Astrological Munchies

-Henry The Hemp

-Zodiacal Roots: The Astrological Soul Of Hemp

- **Green Constellations: Intersection of Hemp and Zodiac**

-Hemp in The Houses: An astrological Adventure Through The Cannabis Galaxy

-Galactic Ganja Guide

Heavenly Hemp
Zodiac Leaves
Doctor Who Astrology
Cannastrology
Stellar Satvias and Cosmic Indicas
Celestial Cannabis: A Zodiac Journey
AstroHerbology: The Sky and The Soil: Volume 1
AstroHerbology:Celestial Cannabis:Volume 2
Cosmic Cannabis Cultivation
The Starry Guide to Herbal Harmony: Volume 1
The Starry Guide to Herbal Harmony: Cannabis Universe: Volume 2
Yugioh Astrology: Astrological Guide to Deck, Duels and more
Nightmare Mansion: Echoes of The Abyss
Nightmare Mansion 2: Legacy of Shadows
Nightmare Mansion 3: Shadows of the Forgotten
Nightmare Mansion 4: Echoes of the Damned
The Life and Banishment of Apophis: Book 2
Nightmare Mansion: Halls of Despair
Healing with Herb: Cannabis and Hydrocephalus
Planetary Pot: Aligning with Astrological Herbs: Volume 1
Fast Track to Freedom: 30 Days to Financial Independence Using AI, Assets, and Agile Hustles
Cosmic Hemp Pathways
How to Become Financially Free in 30 Days: 10,000 Paths to Prosperity
Zodiacal Herbage: Astrological Insights: Volume 1
Nightmare Mansion: Whispers in the Walls
The Daleks Invade Atlantis
Henry the hemp and Hydrocephalus

10X The Kidney Friendly Diet
Cannabis Universe: Adult coloring book

Hemp Astrology: The Healing Power of the Stars

Zodiacal Herbage: Astrological Insights: Cannabis Universe: Volume 2

Planetary Pot: Aligning with Astrological Herbs: Cannabis Universes: Volume 2

Doctor Who: Convergence Protocol – The Replicator War

Nightmare Mansion: Curse of the Blood Moon

The Celestial Stoner: A Guide to the Zodiac

Cosmic Pleasures: Sex Toy Astrology for Every Sign

Hydrocephalus Astrology: Navigating the Stars and Healing Waters

Lapis and the Mischievous Chocolate Bar

Celestial Positions: Sexual Astrology for Every Sign

Apophis's Shadow Work Journal: **:** A Journey of Self-Discovery and Healing

Kinky Cosmos: Sexual Kink Astrology for Every Sign

Digital Cosmos: The Astrological Digimon Compendium

Stellar Seeds: The Cosmic Guide to Growing with Astrology

Apophis's Daily Gratitude Journal

Cat Astrology: Feline Mysteries of the Cosmos

The Cosmic Kama Sutra: An Astrological Guide to Sexual Positions

Unleash Your Potential: A Guided Journal Powered by AI Insights

Whispers of the Enchanted Grove

Cosmic Pleasures: An Astrological Guide to Sexual Kinks

369, 12 Manifestation Journal

Whisper of the nocturne journal(blank journal for writing or drawing)

The Boogey Book

Locked In Reflection: A Chastity Journey Through Locktober

Generating Wealth Quickly:How to Generate $100,000 in 24 Hours

Star Magic: Harness the Power of the Universe

The Flatulence Chronicles: A Fart Journal for Self-Discovery

The Doctor and The Death Moth

Seize the Day: A Personal Seizure Tracking Journal

The Ultimate Boogeyman Safari: A Journey into the Boogie World and Beyond

Whispers of Samhain: 1,000 Spells of Love, Luck, and Lunar Magic: Samhain Spell Book

Apophis's guides:Witch's Spellbook Crafting Guide for Halloween

Frost & Flame: The Enchanted Yule Grimoire of 1000 Winter Spells

The Ultimate Boogey Goo Guide & Spooky Activities for Halloween Fun

Harmony of the Scales: A Libra's Spellcraft for Balance and Beauty

The Enchanted Advent: 36 Days of Christmas Wonders

Nightmare Mansion: The Labyrinth of Screams

Harvest of Enchantment: 1,000 Spells of Gratitude, Love, and Fortune for Thanksgiving

The Boogey Chronicles: A Journal of Nightly Encounters and Shadowy Secrets

The 12 Days of Financial Freedom: A Step-by-Step Christmas Countdown to Transform Your Finances

Sigil of the Eternal Spiral Blank Journal

A Christmas Feast: Timeless Recipes for Every Meal

Holiday Stress-Free Solutions: A Survival Guide to Thriving During the Festive Season

Yu-Gi-Oh! Holiday Gifting Mastery: The Ultimate Guide for Fans and Newcomers Alike

Holiday Harmony: A Hydrocephalus Survival Guide for the Festive Season

Celestial Craft: The Witch's Almanac for 2025 – A Cosmic Guide to Manifestations, Moons, and Mystical Events

Doctor Who: The Toymaker's Winter Wonderland

Tulsa King Unveiled: A Thrilling Guide to Stallone's Mafia Masterpiece

Pendulum Craft: A Complete Guide to Crafting and Using Personalized Divination Tools

Nightmare Mansion: Santa's Eternal Eve

Starlight Noel: A Cosmic Journey through Christmas Mysteries

The Dark Architect: Unlocking the Blueprint of Existence

Surviving the Embrace: The Ultimate Guide to Encounters with The Hugging Molly

The Enchanted Codex: Secrets of the Craft for Witches, Wiccans, and Pagans

Harvest of Gratitude: A Complete Thanksgiving Guide

Yuletide Essentials: A Complete Guide to an Authentic and Magical Christmas

Celestial Smokes: A Cosmic Guide to Cigars and Astrology

Living in Balance: A Comprehensive Survival Guide to Thriving with Diabetes Insipidus

Cosmic Symbiosis: The Venom Zodiac Chronicles

The Cursed Paw of Ambition

Cosmic Symbiosis: The Astrological Venom Journal

Celestial Wonders Unfold: A Stargazer's Guide to the Cosmos (2024-2029)

The Ultimate Black Friday Prepper's Guide: Mastering Shopping Strategies and Savings

Cosmic Sales: The Astrological Guide to Black Friday Shopping

Legends of the Corn Mother and Other Harvest Myths

Whispers of the Harvest: The Corn Mother's Journal

The Evergreen Spellbook

The Doctor Meets the Boogeyman

The White Witch of Rose Hall's SpellBook

The Gingerbread Golem's Shadow: A Study in Sweet Darkness

The Gingerbread Golem Codex: An Academic Exploration of Sweet Myths

The Gingerbread Golem Grimoire: Sweet Magicks and Spells for the Festive Witch

The Curse of the Gingerbread Golem

10-minute Christmas Crafts for kids

Christmas Crisis Solutions: The Ultimate Last-Minute Survival Guide

Gingerbread Golem Recipes: Holiday Treats with a Magical Twist

The Infinite Key: Unlocking Mystical Secrets of the Ages

Enchanted Yule: A Wiccan and Pagan Guide to a Magical and Memorable Season

Dinosaurs of Power: Unlocking Ancient Magick

Astro-Dinos: The Cosmic Guide to Prehistoric Wisdom

Gallifrey's Yule Logs: A Festive Doctor Who Cookbook

The Dino Grimoire: Secrets of Prehistoric Magick

The Gift They Never Knew They Needed

The Gingerbread Golem's Culinary Alchemy: Enchanting Recipes for a Sweetly Dark Feast

A Time Lord Christmas: Holiday Adventures with the Doctor

Krampusproofing Your Home: Defensive Strategies for Yule

Silent Frights: A Collection of Christmas Creepypastas to Chill Your Bones

Santa Raptor's Jolly Carnage: A Dino-Claus Christmas Tale

Prehistoric Palettes: A Dino Wicca Coloring Journey

The Christmas Wishkeeper Chronicles

The Starlight Sleigh: A Holiday Journey

Elf Secrets: The True Magic of the North Pole

Candy Cane Conjurations

Cooking with Kids: Recipes Under 20 Minutes

Doctor Who: The TARDIS Confiscation

The Anxiety First Aid Kit: Quick Tools to Calm Your Mind

Frosty Whispers: A Winter's Tale

The Infinite Key: Unlocking the Secrets to Prosperity, Resilience, and Purpose

The Grasping Void: Why You'll Regret This Purchase

Astrology for Busy Bees: Star Signs Simplified

The Instant Focus Formula: Cut Through the Noise

The Secret Language of Colors: Unlocking the Emotional Codes

Sacred Fossil Chronicles: Blank Journal

The Christmas Cottage Miracle

Feeding Frenzy: Graboid-Inspired Recipes

Manifest in Minutes: The Quick Law of Attraction Guide

The Symbiote Chronicles: Doctor Who's Venomous Journey

Think Tiny, Grow Big: The Minimalist Mindset

The Energy Key: Unlocking Limitless Motivation

New Year, New Magic: Manifesting Your Best Year Yet

Unstoppable You: Mastering Confidence in Minutes

Infinite Energy: The Secret to Never Feeling Drained

Lightning Focus: Mastering the Art of Productivity in a Distracted World

Saturnalia Manifestation Magick: A Guide to Unlocking Abundance During the Solstice

Graboids and Garland: The Ultimate Tremors-Themed Christmas Guide

12 Nights of Holiday Magic

The Power of Pause: 60-Second Mindfulness Practices

The Quick Reset: How to Reclaim Your Life After Burnout

The Shadow Eater: A Tale of Despair and Survival

The Micro-Mastery Method: Transform Your Skills in Just Minutes a Day

Reclaiming Time: How to Live More by Doing Less

Chronovore: The Eternal Nexus

The Mind Reset: Unlocking Your Inner Peace in a Chaotic World
Confidence Code: Building Unshakable Self-Belief
Baby the Vampire Terrier
Baby the Vampire Terrier's Christmas Adventure
Celestial Streams: The Content Creator's Astrology Manual
The Wealth Whisperer: Unlocking Abundance with Everyday Actions
The Energy Equation: Maximize Your Output Without Burning Out
The Happiness Algorithm: Science-Backed Steps to Joyful Living
Stress-Free Success: Achieving Goals Without Anxiety
Mindful Wealth: The New Blueprint for Financial Freedom
The Festive Flavors of New Year: A Culinary Celebration
The Master's Gambit: Keys of Eternal Power
Shadowed Secrets: Groundhog Day Mysteries
Beneath the Burrow: Lessons from the Groundhog
Spring's Whispers: The Groundhog's Prediction
The Limitless Mindset: Unlock Your Untapped Potential
The Focus Funnel: How to Cut Through Chaos and Get Results
Bold Moves: Building Courage to Live on Your Terms
The Daily Shift: Simple Practices for Lasting Transformation
The Quarter-Life Reset: Thriving in Your 20s and 30s
The Art of Shadowplay: Building Your Own Personal Myth
The Eternal Loop: Finding Purpose in Repetition
Burrowing Wisdom: Life Lessons from the Groundhog
Shadow Work: A Groundhog Day Perspective
Love in Bloom: 5-Minute Romantic Gestures
The Shadowspell Codex: Secrets of Forbidden Magick
The Burnout Cure: Finding Balance in a Busy World
The Groundhog Prophecy: Unlocking Seasonal Secrets
Nog Tales: The Spirited History of Eggnog
Six More Weeks: Embracing Seasonal Transitions
The Lumivian Chronicles: Fragments of the Fifth Dimension

Money on Your Mind: A Beginner's Guide to Wealth
The Focus Fix: Breaking Through Distraction
January's Spirit Keepers: Mystical Protectors of the Cold
Creativity Unchained: Unlocking Your Wildest Ideas in 2025
Manifestation Mastery: 365 Days to Rewrite Your Reality
The Groundhog's Mirror: Reflecting on Change
The Weeping Angels' Christmas Curse
Burrowed in Time: A Groundhog Day Journey
Heartbeats: Poems to Share with Your Valentine
Dino Wicca: The Sacred Grimoire of Prehistoric Magick
Courage of the Pride: Finding Your Inner Roar
The Lion's Leap: Bold Moves for Big Results
Healthy Hustle: Achieving Without Overworking
Practical Manifesting: Turning Dreams into Reality in 2025
Jurassic Pharaohs: Unlocking the Magick of Ancient Egypt and Dino Wicca
The Happiness Equation: Small Changes for Big Joy
The Confidence Compass: Finding Your Inner Strength
Whispers in the Hollow: Tales of the Forgotten Beasts
Echoes from the Hollow: The Return of Forgotten Beasts
The Hollow Ascendant: The Rise of the Forgotten Beasts
The Relationship Reset: Building Better Connections
Mastering the Morning: How to Win the Day Before 8 AM
The Shadow's Dance: Groundhog Day Symbolism
Cupid's Kitchen: Quick Valentine's Day Recipes
Valentine's Day on a Budget: Love Without Breaking the Bank
Astrocraft: Aligning the Stars in the World of Minecraft
Forecasting Life: Groundhog Day Reflections
Bleeding Hearts: Twisted Tales of Valentine's Terror
Herbal Smoke Revolution: The Ultimate Guide to Nature's Cigarette Alternative
Winter's Wrath: The Complete Survival Blueprint for Extreme Freezes.

The Groundhog's Shadow: A Tale of Seasons
Burrowed Insights: Wisdom from the Groundhog
Sensual Strings: The Art of Erotic Bondage
Whispered Flames: Unlocking the Power of Fire Play
Forgotten Shadows: A Guide to Cryptids Lost to Time
Six Weeks of Secrets: Groundhog Day's Hidden Messages
Shadows and Cycles: Groundhog Day Reflections
The Art of Love Letters: Crafting the Perfect Message
Romantic Getaways at Home: Turning Your Space into Paradise
Purrfect Brews: A Cat Lover's Guide to Coffee and Companionship
The Groundhog's Wisdom: Timeless Lessons for Modern Life
The Shadow Oracle: Groundhog Day as a Predictor
Emerging from the Burrow: A Journey of Renewal
The Language of Love: Learning Your Partner's Love Style
Authorpreneur: The Ultimate Blueprint for Writing, Publishing, and Thriving as an Author
Weathering the Seasons: Groundhog Day Perspectives
Valentine's Day Magic: A Guide to Romantic Rituals
The Shadow Chronicles: Stories of Groundhog Day
Love and Laughter: Fun Games for Valentine's Day
AstroRealty: Unlocking the Stars for Property Success
The Groundhog's Path: A Guide to Seasonal Balance
Groundhog Day Diaries: Reflections in the Shadow
The Groundhog's Light: Illuminating the Path Ahead
Valentine's Traditions from Around the World
AI Wealth Revolution: Unlocking the Trillionaire Mindset
Love Rekindled: Reigniting Passion in Relationships
Single and Thriving: Self-Love on Valentine's Day
Emerald Legends: Mystical Tales of Ireland
Green Alchemy: Harnessing Nature's Magic
The Hearts of Horror: A Valentine's Day Nightmare

The Leprechaun's Guide to Wealth and Wisdom

Dancing with the Sidhe: Celebrating the Otherworld

Shamrocks and Shadows: Mysteries of the Green Isle

Emerald Energy: Harnessing Luck and Growth

The Gingerbread Golem's Valentine: A Sweetheart's Guide to Love and Enchantment

The Celtic Knot: Weaving Life and Destiny

Green Fire: Elemental Magic for St. Patrick's Day

Clover Chronicles: Finding Your Inner Luck

Ireland's Mystical Creatures: A Field Guide

Gingerbread Golem's Love Almanac

Prowl and Thrive: The Lion's Guide to Success

Love Alchemy: Transforming Your Life Through Heart Energy

WORLD DOMINATION: Woman's Rule 3:The New Life

The Midnight Rose: A Guide to Lunar Love Spells

The Forbidden Letters: Writing Your Own Love Prophecy

Luck and Lore: St. Patrick's Day for Modern Mystics

The Green Path: A Pagan Celebration of Renewal

The Dark Architect's Guide to Reprogramming Reality

Prankster's Paradise: A Guide to Harmless Hijinks

Manifest Your Reality: The Law of Attraction Simplified

The TARDIS Owner's Manual: Understanding the Doctor's Ship: *A complete guide to the TARDIS, its technology, secrets, and mysteries*

Starlit Romance: Astrology Secrets for Finding True Love

The Time Lord's Atlas: A Complete Guide to the Whoniverse: ***A breakdown of the locations, planets, and dimensions explored in Doctor Who***

Sweetheart Shadows: The Dark Side of Love and Attraction

February Fire: Reigniting Passion in Every Area of Life

The Self-Love Toolkit: 5 Ways to Embrace Who You Are

February Sparks: Ignite Your Dreams in 28 Days

March to Success: A 31-Day Action Blueprint
Ancient Paths: The 13 Sacred Principles of Dino Wicca
Echoes of Tomorrow: Navigating the AI Revolution
The Wellness Blueprint: Balancing Mind, Body, and Soul
Green Horizons: Sustainable Living for a Better Tomorrow
The AI Wealth Code: How to Make Millions with Automation
AI-Powered Creativity: Writing, Art, and Music for Profit
Extinction Rites: Rebirthing Your Soul Through Prehistoric Magick
Sacred Serpents tarot
Celestial Enchantment blank journal
Star Strains
Culinary Journeys: Exploring Global Flavors at Home
The Hollowvale Curse
The Hollowvale Harvest
The Egg of Transformation: Awakening Your Inner Power
Blooming Into Power: A Wiccan Guide to Spring Awakening
The Nightmare Nexus: The Third Doctor's Perilous Haunting
Digital Detox: Reclaiming Your Life in a Connected World
Ostara's Path: Walking the Spiral of Renewal
The Sacred Hare
Financial Freedom: Building Wealth in the Modern Age
Spring's Cauldron: Stirring the Waters of Change
The Hollowvale Pact
Quantum Consciousness: The Science of Reality Shifting
The Hollowvale Hunger
The Sacred Waters Within: A Witch's Guide to Hydrocephalus Magick
The Raven's Nest: Building a Life of Unshakable Stability
AI and the Human Mind: The Future of Intelligence
The Hollowvale Reckoning
Timeless Love: Building and Maintaining Lasting Relationships

The Raven's Roar: Unlocking Unstoppable Confidence

Raven Sight: Awakening Intuition and Inner Wisdom

The Butterfly Effect: Small Changes, Big Transformations

Taming the Boogeyman: How to Conquer Your Inner Fears

The Magick of Green: Awakening Earth's Energy in You

The Entrepreneurial Mindset: Secrets to Business Success

The Hollowvale End

The Shadow Luck Ritual: Reclaiming Power from Your Dark Side

Spring Magick for Beginners: A Simple Guide to Seasonal Energy Work

Doctor Who: The Hollowvale Conundrum

The March of Miracles: Unlocking Synchronicities in Spring

Unveiling the Cosmos: A Guide to Stargazing and Space Exploration

The Ultimate Guide to Surviving an Economic Collapse

The AI Gold Rush: How to Profit from the AI Revolution

Bastet's Shadow: The Hidden Power of Feline Magick

The Bastet Codex: Unlocking the Goddess's Magickal Secrets

Purring Spells: Harnessing Bastet's Healing Frequencies

Bastet's Nine Lives: Rebirth, Transformation, and Immortality Spells

Primal Currents: Hydrocephalus Magick in the Path of Dino Wicca

The Digital Gold Rush: Mastering E-Commerce and Online Sales

Future Shock: Adapting to the Next Decade of Change

The Quantum Mindset: Think Like a Billionaire

Sacred Motherhood: Awakening the Divine Feminine Within

The Mother's Spellbook: Enchantments for Love, Protection, and Prosperity

The Witch's Guide to Parenting: Raising Empowered and Intuitive Children

The Magick of Motherhood: Reclaiming Your Power Through Rituals

The Pagan Path to Self-Love: A Goddess's Guide to Worth and Confidence

Wild Woman Magick: Unleashing Your Primal Power

The Money Magnet Blueprint: Unlocking Unlimited Wealth

Biohacking 101: Unlock Your Body's Full Potential

The Wild Father: A Pagan Guide to Strength and Wisdom

The Sacred Masculine: Unlocking Your Inner Power

The Druid's Compass

The Warrior's Mindset

The Father's Fire

Odin's Path

Ancestral Bonds

The House That Whispers

The Magician's Code

The Wild Hunt

The Green Man's Path

The Altar of Success

The Shadow and the Sword

The High Priestess's Guide to Energy Healing

The Lunar Mother

The Sacred Self-Care Grimoire

The Womb Wisdom Codex

The Wheel of the Mother

The Witch's Guide to Manifestation

The Q2 Reset

The Ultimate Guide to AI-Powered Passive Income

Escape the 9-5

AI Feline Fortunes

The Tear-Stained Grimoire

Razorblade Runes

Cemetery Sirens

The Midnight Wristwatch
The Town That Forgets
AI Horror & Creepypasta
The Hollow Frequency
The Breach Echo
The Quiet Between Worlds
The Sigil of Tharan-Khul
Summon the Vault of Y'ha'ten
The Becoming Codex
The Profit of Az'ra-nar
The Drowned Logos
Echoes of the Eldritch Will
The Deep Ledger
Necronomicon of Networth
Covenant of the Wealthwyrm
The Whisperer's Manifesto
The Rites of Azh-K'luth
The Ark of the Crawling Coin
The Tithe of Shadows
Inkheart Abyss
The Timewinds of Y'ha-nthlei
The Spiral Labyrinth of Azag-Nirrh
The Gallifreyan Heresy of the Black Pharaoh
The Psalms of Nyog-Sotha
Black Rain Alchemy
The Infinite Maw
The Entropic Blueprint
The Oracle of Sh'guul
The Book of Breach
The Drowned Saint's Testament
Dreamcraft of the Sleeper God
The Silence Market
Cthonomics: The Dark Wealth Algorithm

Invocation of the Ten-Eyed King
Wealthbound to the Wyrm Below
Become the Unnameable
Codex of the Sovereign Flame
Rituals of Relentless Becoming
The Shadow Ascends
The Eyes Beneath You
The Will That Wakes Worlds
Silence Is a Weapon
The Mirror That Screams
The Whisper Between Moments
The Mind That Devours Fear
The Myth of the Finished Self
The Architect of Your Madness
The Voice You've Buried
The Discipline of Madness
Stormborn: Awakening Your Inner Tempest
The Mind That Ate Time
Unbind Your Becoming
The Pact You Owe Yourself
The Devourer's Diet
The Acid That Carves the Path
The Tower You Must Burn
The Breath Between Worlds
Speak Like the Deep
The Labyrinth Within
The Spine of the Sea God
Rejection Is a Portal
The Crown You Refused
The Scar Is the Spell
The Lightless Flame
The Habit of Becoming Horrific
ChickenJockey Chaos

The Gatekeeper Within
You Are Not Your Name
The Compass of the Mad
The Archive of Unsent Letters
What the Mirror Can't Show You
The Knife You Needed
Worship Nothing, Become Everything
The Other Voice
The Body the World Forgot
The Vein of the Void
The Black Bone Codex
The Puzzle of the Hidden Self (Millennium Puzzle)
The Eye That Sees the Lie *(Millennium Eye)*
The Ring of Return (Millennium Ring)
The Rod of Relentless Will ***(Millennium Rod)***
The Tally of the Soul (Millennium Tauk/Necklace)
The Key to the Locked Timeline (Millennium Key)
The Scale of Sacred Decisions (Millennium Scales)
Inferno Bites: The UnOfficial Minecraft Lava Cookbook
Rot in the Attic
Prana: The Hidden Force of Your Infinite Self
The Shadow Realm Within: Transforming Darkness Into Destiny
The Borderland Collapse
Claws of Protection: Bastet's Defensive Magick
Mr. Ring-a-Ding's Madness
Yugioh Astrology: Celestial Deckcraft and Duel Destiny (2026–2027 Edition)
The Seal You Signed: Unlocking the Power You Once Feared
The Puzzle of Infinite Minds: Unlocking the Mentalism Hidden Within
The Eye That Mirrors the All: Secrets of Inner Reflection
Doctor Who: The Toymaker's Broadcast

Rootwake: The Carbon Covenant
Skitter Logic: Unlearning the Fear That Built You
Doctor Who: The World That Froths
Rootwake: The Fizz That Rewrites Flesh
Rootwake: Frothfather of the World
The Holly Pact: Blood Beneath the Mistletoe
The 2nd Mass Principle: Building Unbreakable Tribes
Web of Wits: A Survival Guide to Encounters with Anasi the Spider (Aunt Nancy)
The Hexbreaking Handbook: Effective Spells to Remove Curses
Pop Alchemy: Transform Your Life One Sip at a Time
The Mason Code: Leading in Unleadable Times
Petosiris and the Fifth Chamber of Thoth
The Ether Seed Within
The Parent of Tomorrow
Petosiris's Pyramid of Perpetual Wealth
Unlearn the World
Grimoire of the Hollow Tongue
Zodiac Weeds: Finding Your Strain Through the Stars
Aquarius Rises in the Bank
The Sugar God's Smile
The Skinclock Reversal: Biohacking the Face of Time
Debtburn: How to Obliterate What You Owe Forever
The Ice Cream Oracle: What Your Cone Says About Your Future
Silence Is Sovereignty: The Power of Being Unreadable
The Wind That Whispers Through Stone
Path of the Four Directions
Doctor Who: The Maestro's Symphony of Endings
Oxygen Grail: Breathing to Undo the Clock
Zodiacal Collapse: When Stars Devour Time
Teachings from the Red Sand Silence

Doctor Who: Omega – The Broken Equation
Memory Wipe Your Past: Start Over Like a MiB
Mitochondria Prime: Ignite the Core of Youth
A Nest of Roaches
Grub from the Galaxy: MiB Recipes You'll Never Forget
Whiskers of Power: Bastet's Guide to Inner Sovereignty
The Gift Must Cost Them: Negotiation Through Unequal Exchange
The Worm Guys' Wealth Code: Hustle Like an Alien
Bug Out: The Edgar Method for Ruthless Goal Setting
Weaving Life with Spiderwoman's Pattern
Doctor Who: The Rani's Renaissance
How to Get a Job (If You're a Puppygirl)
Speak Through Others: The Art of Proxy Power
T-Rex Your Trauma: Reclaim the Power of Your Primal Self
The Black Briefcase: How MiB Stay Wealthy in Silence
The Thirst Beyond Reason: Understanding Diabetes Insipidus From the Inside Out
Backwoods Witchcraft for Billionaires: The Pagan Path from Dirt Roads to Gold Roads
The Moonshine Grimoire: Fermented Spells for Abundance
The Nameless Geometry
The Wraith's Mixtape: Spellcasting with Songs of Sorrow
The Gallifreyan Gentleman: Silent Wealth, Sonic Confidence, and the Doctor's Code of Living
Sugar Water Confidence
Dino Totems: Spirit Guides from Earth's First Gods
Pumpkin Sigils & Ritual Smoke
The Hózhó Compass
The Distortus Discipline – Order from Inner Mutation
Witchcraft for the Cold-Blooded Soul
Moonlight Over the Blessingway
Water, Interrupted: When the Body Forgets How to Hold On

Deformed but Divine: Embracing Your Asymmetry

Hexes in the Henhouse: The Farm Witch's Guide to Power

The Reversed Flame: A Grimoire of Inverted Power

Salt, Cells, and Sanity: Reclaiming Balance with Diabetes Insipidus

King of the Broken: Crowning the Flawed Self

Moonlight Scars: Emo Moon Magick and the Art of Lunar Sorrow

Noose Spells: Magick of the Hanging Rope

The Goth Cathedral: Rituals of the Broken and Beautiful

The Cretaceous Codex: Dino Spirits and Fossil Magick

The Turkey Bones Ritual

Nine Lives of Manifestation: Unlocking Bastet's Reality Codes

Chaos Muscles: Building Strength from Twisted Pain

Emo Blood Magick: The Veins of Power

The 3AM Flood: Nighttime Urination, Sleep Loss, and the DI Spiral

The Silence Between the Stars

The Lemon Method: Sour Your Way to Success

Starlit Sovereign

The Rite of Twelve Gates: Walking the Gates of the Duat.

Cornbread and Conjure: Recipes for Riches and Rootwork

The Black Rose Rituals: Emo Love Spells and Obsession Magick

The Eternal Goodbye: Death Magick and Rebirth Rituals

Sinkrot: The Drain That Remembers

The Hybrid Mindset: Thinking Beyond Evolution

Bone Dry: Navigating Dehydration Before It Breaks You

Wreathcraft: Winter Sigils and Yuletide Spells

The Rite of Twelve Mouths

S'mores of the Damned: Haunted Recipes for Halloween Night

Rethink the Drink: A Beverage Survival Guide for DI Warriors

The Shadow Chord: Guitar Magick and Sonic

Malformed Yet Majestic: Leading When You Feel Wrong Inside

The Cursed Diary: Ink-Stained Spells of the Emo Soul

Anxiety Off Switch: Emergency Reset for a Fried Nervous System

The Energy Heist: How to Take Back Your Life from Drainers

Beyond the Bathroom: Rebuilding Your Social Life With DI

Coyote's Gift for Decision Makers

Ghoul-Goo: Spooky S'mores You'll Die For

Echoes in the Mirror: Scrying and Self-Destruction Magick

Thread and Thorn: Stitching Spells from Rural Cloth

The Mogwai Mind: Building Untouchable Wealth from Small Ideas

Be Your Own Guide: Trust Your Inner Compass

Hormones in Chaos: The Endocrine Puzzle of Diabetes Insipidus

ChronoCleanse: Detox Your Biological Timeline

The Limb You Hide Is the One That Saves You

Leaves, Bones, and Whisper Spells

The Dinosaur Mindset: Prehistoric Tactics for Modern Wealth

Clawing Back Control: A Bastet Method for Boundaries and Empowerment

Samhain Codes of the Forgotten

Orange Alchemy: The Autumnal Spellbook

Monster Within, Master Without

The Sigil That Sleeps

Hearthcraft: Yule Hearth Sigils and Winter Warmth Spells

Temple of the Purring Moon: Rituals from Bastet's Lineage

When the Earth Remembers Your Footsteps

Food for Mood: Eat to Heal Depression, Not Just Survive It
Witch of the Kudzu Vine: Southern Pagan Wealth Secrets
The Invisible Diagnosis: Advocating for Yourself With DI
The Coffin's Lullaby: Sleep Magick and Nightmares as Portals
Ashes of the Will: Rituals for Erasing the Self
The Fracture Rite: Shattering the Magickal Core
Funeral Candles: The Art of Emo Flame Magick
The Black Grimoire: A Blank Ritual for Writing in Absence
Phantom Thirst: A Halloween Survival Guide for Diabetes Insipidus
The Hollow Crown: Emo Royalty and Magick of the Outcast King
Sandpainting for the Soul
Falling Into Balance: Using the Extra Hour to Recalibrate Life
100 Southern Superstitions That Still Work
The DI Child: A Parent's Guide to Raising Hydrated, Happy Kids
The Jungle of Shame: Escaping the Hidden Lab of Doubt
The Witch's Toast: S'mores Spells and Creepy Confections
The Hoodoo Pantry: Spells from the Mason Jar
The Immortal Fortune: Secret Wealth Lessons from Captain Jack Harkness
The Specter's Embrace: Magick for Channeling Ghostly Lovers
Grateful Waters: A Thanksgiving Survival Guide for Diabetes Insipidus
The Seizure Gospel
Harvestbind: Autumn Sigils and Samhain Spells
Doctor Who: The Algorithmic Awakening
Silent Nights, Steady Waters: A Christmas Survival Guide for Diabetes Insipidus
The Extra Hour Effect: How One Hour Can Transform Everything

Blade Between the Breaths
Running with the Mountain Shadows
Echoes of the Failed Experiment – Becoming a Living Legacy
Swamp Witches & River Ghosts: Real Southern Hauntings
Cornbread Prophecies: Magical Recipes from a Southern Table
Doctor Who: The Signal in the Star
Bloomcraft: Spring Sigils and Equinox Enchantments
Vanisher: How to Disappear from the Internet Without Losing Your Life
The Ultimate Christmas Cookie Cookbook
The Unbreakable Parent: How to Mentally Survive Raising Kids in a Broken World
Time Debt: How to Reclaim the Hours You Didn't Know You Lost
One Month, One Million: Unconventional Cash Creation Tactics
Doctor Who: The Cyber Conversion Protocol
Black Friday Frenzy: The Art of Finding Hidden Online Deals
The Grimoire Buried Under the Apple Tree
Digital Couponing Masterclass: Your Step-by-Step Guide to Black Friday Savings
The Fire Inside the Flint
Shadows on the Ceiling: The Emo Guide to Astral Magick
The Bone-Eaters Beneath Us
Black Friday Bundle Blueprint: Creating Irresistible Product Packages for Maximum Sales
Thirteen Nights of Unbinding
Doctor Who: Engines of Influence
Pumpkin Spice Alchemy: Recipes of Fire and Frost
When Raptor Met Rexy: Prehistoric Lessons in Wild Romance
Oblivion's Candle: Burn the Path Behind You

Campfire Curses and Chocolate: A Halloween S'mores Grimoire

The Wallet That Wasn't Mine: Breaking Free from Inherited Scarcity

The Cola Zodiac: What Your Fizz Says About Your Fate

Frostfire Fortune: Unlocking Winter's Hidden Prosperity

Signal Jamming: Detox Your Brain from Info Overload

The Dust of the Forgotten Rite

The Golden Cat Sigils: Drawing Power in Bastet's Name

Mud Magick: The Prosperity of Getting Dirty

Savory Spicefall: Beyond the Pumpkin Pie

Pumpkin Spice Apothecary Kitchen

The Pumpkin Spice Economy: Turning Trends into Billions

The Ember Veil: 13 Nights of Fire Magick

Financial Freeze: When Earning Triggers Panic

The Gingerbread Alchemist: Sweet Recipes with a Twist

Biosynth Power: Programming Yourself from Scratch

Echoes from the Talking Circle

Truffle Alchemy: Fungus of Fortune

Spores of Power: The Truffle Witch's Handbook

Doctor Who: The Tower That Speaks

The Mycelium Veil: Truffle Magick Unbound

Broke But Ashamed: Healing the Shame Wound of Debt

The Evergreen Mind: Growth Through Winter Stillness

The Black Veil Truffle Rite

The Voice Beneath Symbols

Witchlight on the Bayou: Swamp Spells for Sovereignty

I Grew Up Poor and Now I Sabotage My Success

The Lantern of Hollow Souls

Shutdown Survival: A Citizen's Guide to Thriving When Government Stops

When Abundance Feels Like a Threat: Healing the Hidden Fears of Enough

The Scarecrow Grimoire
Owls of the October Veil
Candlewax and Curses: A Halloween Spellbook
Excavating the Inner Fossil – Transforming Fossilized Thoughtforms into Tools of Power
The Yule Witch's Spellbook: Magick for the Holiday Season
Haunted Christmas: Ghost Stories for Winter Nights
The Christmas Survival Guide: Thriving Through the Chaos
The Bone Orchard Rites
Haunted Commerce: The Ghost in the Marketplace
When Money Triggers the Inner Child
Silent Night with the Silence: A Christmas Thriller
The Lightning Crown: Living and Leading Through Seizures
TARDIS Tidings: Festive Stories from the Whoniverse
Autumn Reset: Slowing Down Without Falling Behind
The Trillion Dollar Soul: Rewriting the Currency of Reality
Truffle Eclipse Magick
Micro-Manifestations: Quick Magick That Works
5-Minute Rituals for Busy Witches
The Marshmallow Massacre: Halloween Treats with a Sinister Twist
Blood and Blackberry Thorns
Magickal Mornings: Rituals for a Blessed Christmas Day
Embers of the All-Hallows Fire
The Pumpkin Market Collapse
The Hour You Gained: Transforming Time Into Power
The Chamber Must Be Sealed: Mastering the Power of Controlled Access
The Cursed Manuscript of Petosiris
The Festive Hearth: Creating Holiday Traditions
Darkness Rising: Thriving as Nights Grow Longer
Harvesting Time: Turning the Year's End Into Your New Beginning

Petosiris and the 13th Zodiac Key

Wagewound: When Paychecks Become Identity Prisons

Walls That Watch

The Silent Feast: Rituals of Power in the Longest Night

The Distortus Legacy : Becoming a Deformed King in a Perfect World

The Hollow Masks

The Gratitude Furnace: Forging Gold from Thanks

Feast of Inner Gold: Eating for Energy and Enlightenment

Haunted Commerce: The Season of Spending Spirits

Fear Bonds: How Panic Creates Profit

Black Friday E-Commerce Playbook: Sales Tactics to Skyrocket Your Holiday Revenue

Budgeting for Black Friday: A Holiday Savings Planner

Haunting the Harvest Moon

The Warrior's Water: Emergency Preparedness for People With DI

The First Sip of the Year: A New Year's Survival Guide for Diabetes Insipidus

Doctor Who: The Thirteenth Node

The Unseen Struggle: Mental Health, Anxiety, and Chronic Thirst

The Hearth's Hidden Ledger: Counting Energies as Currency

The Gift Alchemist: Turning Any Offering Into Gold

The Papyrus of the Bound Spirit

The Magick of Leftovers: Transmutation in the Fridge

Frost and Fortune: Christmas Wealthcraft for the Modern Magus

Last-Minute Gifts: Creative Ideas on a Budget

10 Secrets to Surviving Holiday Crowds

The Witch's Dow Jones

The Witches' Graveyard Shift

Pumpkin Sigils: Carving Rites for Midnight Power

The Secret Shopper's Black Friday Guide: How to Get Early Access and VIP Deals

Fever in the Foundation

The Neuralyzer Reset: Reprogram Your Morning Routine

Lightning Lessons of the White Painted Woman

The Enchanted Snowflake

The Magic Sip: Surviving Disney Parks with Diabetes Insipidus

The One Who Draws Through You

Santa's Secrets: A Magical Holiday Planner

Silent Bells, Loud Miracles: Self-Help for the Season of Stillness

The Sugar Spell Codex: Confectionary Magick of Christmas

Autumn Hexcraft: Fallen Leaves, Fallen Barriers

Sleep Like a Fortress: Build a Life Where Insomnia Can't Survive

Nowhere Was Ever Home

Christmas Under the Stars: A Celestial Holiday Guide

Rentproof: How to Never Be Evicted Again

Workless: Escape the 9-5 Without Being Broke

The Gilded Gift: A Wealth Altar for Christmas Morning

The Black Friday Grimoire

The Hollowing: Ceremonies of Spiritual Collapse

Doctor Who: The Nameless Signal

Where the Eagle Hides His Courage

The Dwarf Tyrant's Ascent: Claiming Power in a World of Giants

The Currency of the Dead: Trading with Spectral Bankers

The Icebound Witch: Survival and Magick in the Cold

The Emergency Money Mind: Constant Crisis, Zero Calm

Thirst & Roses: A Valentine's Survival Guide for Diabetes Insipidus

Springing Into Clarity: Mastering the Energy Shift of Daylight Saving

Speed of the Nanotyrant: Agile Strategies for Life's Hunt

The 90-Day Reset: A Science-Backed Guide to Reinvent Yourself Before the New Year

The Coil of Thorns

Timegates Unleashed

Dopamine Fasting 2.0: Rewiring Your Brain in a World of Overstimulation

The Nanotyrannus Mutation: Embracing Your Differentiated Form

Unwritten January: How to Use the Blank Page of the Year to Re-Author Your Life

Feast of the Forgotten Spirits: Ancestor Magick for the Holidays

The Burnout Codex: A System for Thriving Beyond Stress

I Don't Deserve to Have Money

When the King Doesn't See You: The Shadow Predator's Guide

The Reset Ritual :A Guide to Shedding Last Year's Weight—Emotional and Physical—by Spring Cleaning Your Soul

Calendar Alchemy: Learn to Bend Time and Productivity around Your Natural Rhythms

The Mirror Contract: A One-Sentence Agreement with Yourself that Unlocks Real Change

The Nile Formula: Sacred Flow for Millionaire Minds

Forward Momentum: Productivity Rituals for the Lost Hour

Harvest Gold: Wealth Magick of Pumpkin Spice Commerce

The Magick of Christmas Lights: Illuminating Holiday Rituals

Cranberry Crown: Royal Self-Worth through Ritual Meals

Petosiris and the Worms of the Feathered Throne

The Evergreen Equation: Self-Help for Sustained Growth

The Rain Will Wash Us Away: Emo Weather Magick

Snowlight Shadows: Magick Under Frozen Stars

Doctor Who: Merger of Empires

The Light Within the Feast: Magickal Wealth of Yuletide Flame

Momentum Machines: Small Habits Designed to Snowball into Unstoppable Forward Motion

Calm Spells: Magickal Solutions for Anxiety Relief

Santa's Final List: The Naughty Never Leave

The Mystic's Guide to Banishing Worry

The Silence Dividend: Turning Quiet Mornings into Compounding Growth All Year

Charmed Stillness: Rituals to Ease the Mind

Blood Spiral Ascension

The Vanishing Heart Invocation

Crystal Calm: Harnessing Stones for Anxiety

The Nano Tyrant Code: Strength in the Small Predator

The Energy Ledger: Accounting Methods for Vitality, Not Just Money

Snowglobe Mindset: Shake Up Your Thoughts, Settle Into Peace

The Weight of the Feather: Anubis's Codes for Soul Balance

Pocket Peppermint Power: Tiny Rituals for Big Holiday Energy

Shadowkeeper of the Golden Jackal: Anubis's Path to Energetic Protection

The Witch's Breath: Anxiety Relief Through Magickal Breathing

The Tiny Ember: Pocket Motivation for Cold Days

Stocking Sorcery: Mini Spells for Holiday Luck and Prosperity

Warm Hands, Steady Heart: Micro Grounding for Winter Anxiety

The Fourteenth Doctor: A New Beginning (David Tennant, 2022–2023)

The Fifteenth Doctor: Rewriting the Stars
(Ncuti Gatwa, 2023–2025)

Santa's Shortcut to Success: Micro Habits for a Better New Year

The Midnight Cocoa Manifesto: Comfort Rituals for Hard Nights

Why I Can't Save: Trauma Blocks to Financial Planning

Dino Brain, Mega Goals: Rewire Yourself for Savage Success.

Jurassic Profit: Unearth Your Inner Millionaire Fossil

Scales & Softness: Dating with Dino Heart

Carnotaurus Dreams.

Red Willow Thinking.

Reindeer Resilience: How to Keep Going When You're Exhausted

Candlewick Courage: Lighting Strength in Dark Seasons.

Elf-Mode Focus: Fast Attention Fixes for Busy Seasons

Futureproof Feelings: Emotional Skill-Building for Resilience No Matter What the New Year Brings

The 90-Day Rewire: Transform Your Neural Pathways Before Spring Blooms

Jolly Rich: Christmas Micro-Money Magick for Fast Prosperity.

Gingerbread Gratitude: Mini Practices for a Happier Holiday

Trauma-Spending: When Money Becomes a Drug

Goal Skeletons: Build Minimalist Frameworks for Resolutions That Last

The Snarl Strategy: Growling Back at a World That Silenced You

The Hourglass Reset: Reclaiming What the Clock Took

Yule Claw: Dino Rites of Light in the Darkness

Sacred Circles: Grounding Rituals for Anxious Souls

Clockstopper's Gut: Rebuilding the Core of Time

Winterfire Drive: Harness the Cold Season's Stillness to Ignite Deep Motivation

The 5-Minute Productivity Hack: Small Steps to Big Results

Light Ascending: A Self-Help Guide to Longer Days

Inner Economy: Trade Self-Doubt for Confidence Like a High-Value Currency

Simple Success: Decluttering Your Life for Better Results

The Resilient Mind: Thriving in Tough Times

The 2026 Playbook: Mastering the Year Ahead

The Spring Sleep Solution: Conquering Fatigue After Time Change.

The Hormonal Compass: Navigate Back to Your Youth

Golden Vision: Eating for Your Eye Color with the Power of Ghee

Lionhearted Love: Strength in Relationships

MiB Mindset: Think Like a Cosmic Agent

The Ladder of Small Wins: Climb Out of Stagnation by Stacking Micro-Victories

The Momentum Hour: Gaining More in Less Time.

The Year of You: A Self-Help Blueprint for Unapologetic Self-Ownership

The Dust That Watches You Back.

The Astral Parent

Shadow of the King: The Nanotyrannus Parable

Tiny Tidings of Triumph: Small Wins That Change Your Life

Dwarf Tyrant Rising: When You're the One They Overlook

The Bank Account Mirror: Healing How You See Yourself Through Money

Cretaceous Black

When Love Costs Too Much: Romantic Triggers and Financial Wounds

Dream-Eater's Guide to Wealth

Unzipped Reality: The Jacket That Opens Portals

The Power of No: How to Set Boundaries and Get Rich

Keeper of the Desert Veil: Anubis's Teachings on Illusion & Truth

Redacted Stargates: Stories the SGC Buried

The Clock That Dripped Time

Doctor Who: The Silent Acquisition

Hairline Manifestation: Unlocking Power at the Edge of Thought

Cash-Eater Crickets: How Insects Predict Economic Collapse

Dead Pet Whisperer: Grief Alchemy from the Other Side

The Love Algorithm Is Broken: Hack Romance Before It Hacks You

The Rite of the 8-Limbed Seal

Melt the Moon: A Fire Ritual to Reshape Emotion

Venomous Miracles: Healing Through the Poison Path

Wealth Without Water: The Post-Aquatic Rich Life

The Butterfly Betrayal: When Change Turns on You

The Quiet Upgrade: How Humans Are Secretly Rebuilding Themselves Without Asking Permission

Nobody Taught Us This: The Missing Human Manual for Money, Energy, and Self-Respect

You Were Never Broken: Why Most People Are Reacting Normally to an Unstable World

After the Noise Ends: How Humans Reset When the World Finally Goes Quiet

The Month That Tells the Truth: Why January Reveals What the Rest of the Year Hides

Tremors Party Unleashed: The Ultimate Guide to a Graboids Birthday Bash

Cold Start Human: Rebooting Motivation Without Forcing Momentum

The Year that doesn't start until they say

Love Without Performance: What Connection Looks Like When No One Is Watching

February Is a Mirror: What Love Exposes About You

How We Learned Love Wrong: Uninstalling Cultural Myths About Connection

You Are Not Too Much: Why Needing Love Is Not a Flaw

The Crooked Fence Covenant: Backwoods Boundaries and Witch Wealth

The Day That Keeps Repeating: Why Your Life Feels Stuck—and How to Shift It Gently

Nothing Changes Until Something Softens: Escaping Repetition Without Violence to Yourself

Same Life, Different Ending: How Tiny Choices Rewrite Repetition

The Loop Isn't Punishment: Why You're Being Asked to Learn, Not Suffer

Panic at the Register: Retail Anxiety and Public Shame

The Secret Formula to Becoming an Influencer in 90 Days

The New Rich: How to Retire by 35

Digital Nomad Secrets: How to Travel the World and Make Millions

Burn Your Waiting Room: Escape the Delay Spiral

Strapped for Pleasure: A Complete Guide to Pegging and Strap-On Play

Locked in Desire: A Guide to Chastity Play and Intimate Control

Burrowing into History: Groundhog Day Through the Ages

The Shadow Forecast: The Science of Groundhog Day

Choice Cascades: How One Decision in January Sets Ripples for the Whole Year

The Anti-Anxiety Blueprint: Mastering Fear and Stress for Success

The Ancestral Path of the Jackal Priest

Winterborn Titans: Giants of Ice and Stone
The Extinction Spire
The Emotion That Made Me Millions
Delete Their Voice: Become Unreachable
The Frostbound Mysteries: Mythical Beings of January's Chill
The Roar Within: Unlocking Your Potential
From Burrow to Sky: Groundhog Day Explained
The Boogey Book: Festive Ward-Off Edition
Fooled Ya! The Psychology Behind Great Pranks
April Fools' Alchemy: Transforming Everyday Items into Pranks
Anchor Habits: Root Yourself in Unshakable Routines That Endure Seasonal Change
Emerald Waters: A St. Patrick's Day Survival Guide for Diabetes Insipidus
The Groundhog's Legacy: Myths, Legends, and Facts
Six Weeks of Mystery: The Truth Behind Groundhog Day
The Upgrade Mind: Tech-Like Patches and Updates for Your Mental Operating System
Moon Blood, Star Flesh: Embracing Your Hybrid Nature
Groundhog Lore and Legend: A Complete Guide
You Are the Lie They Can't Kill
Download a Different Reality
The Quiet Advantage: Winning Without Announcing Yourself
A Year of Gratitude: Unlocking Joy
Touch Grass: A Pagan Reset for a Burned-Out Digital World
Cold Start Wealth: Building Financial Power from a Standing Still Point
Astrology Without Fate: Using Cycles Without Surrendering Control
The Future is Remote: Work Less, Earn More, Live Anywhere
Harvest of Silence

The Algorithm Knows Your Name
April Fools' Day for Introverts
Soft Power Systems: Influence That Doesn't Exhaust You
Practical Magick for Real Life: Focus, Intent, and Follow-Through
January Is a Lie: Designing Momentum Without the Calendar
Universal Flow: Managing DI in High-Energy Theme Parks
Electric Allure: Exploring Erotic Electro-Play
The Masked Embrace: Exploring Sensory Deprivation
The Ultimate April Fools' Survival Guide
Splashproof Survival: Waterparks & Wave Pools with DI
Agile Predator, Still King: Crafting Your Speed in a World That Celebrates Size
The Shadow Feast: Groundhog Day's Sinister Side
The Bug's Business Model
Edge of Bliss: Mastering the Art of Tease and Denial
Midnight Alchemy: Rituals for Transformation Between the Old Year and the New
Punxsutawney Bloodlines: A Groundhog Day Horror
The Burrower: Groundhog Day's Darkest Secrets
Buried Alive: A Groundhog Day Horror Story
Blood Moon Markets: The Witch's Guide to Wealth Magick
The Groundhog's Shadow: What It Means for the World
Seasonal Shadows: The Groundhog Day Phenomenon
The Shadow's Curse: A Groundhog Day Horror Tale
Punxsutawney Revealed: A Guide to Groundhog Day
Safari Hydration: Zoo & Wildlife Park Survival for DI
The Foolproof Prank Planner
***Latex Lust: Embracing Fetish Fashion* is a sophisticated**
Whip & Whisper: The Dynamics of Impact Play
The Shadow Burrow Chronicles: Horror Beneath the Ground
Frozen Shadows: A Groundhog Day Thriller
The Groundhog's Revenge: A February Nightmare

Burrow of the Damned
Everyday Enchantment: Magickal Practices for Modern Living
Budget Bliss: The Easy Path to Financial Freedom
Six More Weeks of Terror
The Oxygen Debt
The Ice Veil: Mystical Beasts of January's Shadows
Roots That Remember
Polar Myths: Creatures of the Icy Abyss
The Marginalia Covenant
AI and the Occult: Digital Spirits, Sigils, and Cyber-Witchcraft
Roleplay Realms: Crafting Fantasies and Scenes
The Last Clean River
Lover in the Shadows: A Groundhog Day Tale
Buried Hearts: A Groundhog Day Gothic Romance
Anubis Wept for Petosiris
The Lantern Knows Your Name
Rituals of the Last Shadow
The Bell That Rings for No One
Shadows of Love and Death
The Groundhog's Bride: A Dark Valentine's Tale
Frozen Kisses: A Horror Romance for Groundhog Day
The Creative Spark: Igniting Your Passion Projects
From Cub to King: A Journey of Transformation
Six Weeks to Midnight: A Groundhog Day Romance
Tide of the Unclean
Burrow of Desire: A Groundhog Day Paranormal Romance
The Shadow Magick Almanac: Harnessing Groundhog Day Energies
AI for Emo Influencers: Growing an Online Following Without the Anxiety
AI for the Melancholy Millionaire: Making Money Without Social Interaction

Winter's Grip: A Horror Romance Beneath the Frost
Shadowed Hearts: A Love Buried in Winter's Chill
The Shadow Lover: A Groundhog Day Gothic Love Story
Beneath the Burrow: A Groundhog Day Thriller
The Punxsutawney Conspiracy
The Crimson Pact: Emo Blood Oath Magick
The Shadows of Gallifrey: A Doctor Who Horror Collection
Whispers in the Vortex: Chilling Tales from the TARDIS
AI Ghostwriting for Emo Souls: How to Make Money Writing Without Trying
The Anti-Social Emo's Guide to AI-Powered Freelancing
Emo AI Therapy: Talking to Robots When Humans Suck
Cry & Collect: AI-Powered Passive Income for Emos
The Weeping Angel Chronicles: A Collection of Terror
Dating Without the Mask
The Clockwork Menace: Horror Stories from the Future
Tender Doesn't Mean Weak
Not a Burden, Not a Bonus
Dalek Nightmares: Stories of Ultimate Extermination
The Empty Child's Curse: Tales of Horror and Fear
The TARDIS Ghost Files: Hauntings Across the Universe
Soft Armor, Open Heart
Chosen Gently
Love That Doesn't Rush You
Financial Gaslighting: When You're Made to Feel Crazy About Money.
After the Bees Went Silent
The Soil Knows Your Name
The Quantum Magick Codex: Unlocking the Hidden Laws of Reality
The Gingerbread Golem's Awakening: A Tale of Sweet Revenge

The Gingerbread Golem Chronicles: Guardians of Frost Hollow
The Power of Focus: Eliminate Distractions, Achieve Greatness
Sacred Submission: The Dynamics of D/s Relationships
The Magick of Numbers: Unlocking the Hidden Codes of the Universe
Blood and Bones: The Ancient Magick of Life and Death
Doctor Who: The Collapse Dividend
Thesis of the Unremembered
Desired as You Are
The Energy Budget of Love
Romancing Your Potential: The Love Month Growth Guide
Seen, Not Studied
Screams from the Void: Horror Stories Inspired by Doctor Who
The Silence Is Watching: A Collection of Dread
Under the Floorboards
The House of Feathers and Fangs
Emperor Bones, Hollow Crown
Goreglyphs of the Boiling Deep
The Coven That Screamed Back
The Stacks That Breathe
Love That Adapts
Nightmares on Gallifrey: Frights from the Doctor Who Universe
Apache Ways to Heal Powerfully
Belos Left No Corpses
The Algorithm Hates You (Good.)
Starve the Soul, Feed the Flame
Romance Without Apology
The Carbon Illusion
Your Nervous System is Your GPS

Where Rest Learns Your Name: Six Gentle Bedtime Stories for Minds That Work Differently

Soft Armor for Tender Nights: Six 5-Minute Bedtime Stories for Hearts That Have Been Hurt

Paws of Night, Path of Stars: Six 5-Minute Bedtime Stories Guided by Bastet and Anubis

When the Mind Needs a Lamp: Six 5-Minute Bedtime Stories for Gentle Mental Health Care

Imbolc Roar: Awakening the Dino Flame

The Titan Never Died

Witchflesh Harvest

Become the Thought They Can't Unsee

Golden Threads: The Sensuality of Body Worship

Chains of Desire: Exploring the Beauty of Restraint

Glyphs Written in Organs

Living Below the Line

Palismen Don't Scream—Until They Do

The Boiling Isles Devour the Weak

Hexside Anatomy Lab

Philip Wittebane and the First Body

www.ingramcontent.com/pod-product-compliance
Lightning Source LLC
LaVergne TN
LVHW022231200926
848481LV00006B/2228
9798295605147